101 Seeds *for* Library Joy

ALA Editions purchases fund advocacy,
awareness, and accreditation programs
for library professionals worldwide.

101 Seeds *for* Library Joy

REBECCA HASS

ALA Editions
Chicago 2025

Rebecca Hass (she/her/hers) is the programming and out-reach manager for Anne Arundel County Public Library (AACPL). Prior to AACPL, she served in librarianship and management with the Enoch Pratt Free Library and Ramsey County Public Library. Rebecca received her MLIS from Dominican University in 2008 and her Life and Engagement Coaching Certificate from Anne Arundel Community College in 2022. Rebecca integrates positive psychology practices with DEIB approaches in libraries, community engagement, coaching, and consulting in her business, Joy Work, LLC., http://joyworkllc.com.

Extensive effort has gone into ensuring the reliability of the information in this book; however, the publisher makes no warranty, express or implied, with respect to the material contained herein.

ISBN: 979-8-89255-587-6 (paper)

Library of Congress Cataloging-in-Publication Data
Names: Hass, Rebecca, author.
Title: 101 seeds for library joy / Rebecca Hass.
Other titles: One hundred one seeds for library joy
Description: Chicago : ALA Editions, 2025. | Includes bibliographical references.
Identifiers: LCCN 2024026063 | ISBN 9798892555876 (paperback)
Subjects: LCSH: Librarians—Psychology. | Library employees—Psychology. | Work environment—Psychological aspects. | Joy.
Classification: LCC Z682.35.P82 H37 2024 | DDC 020.92—dc23/eng20240916
LC record available at https://lccn.loc.gov/2024026063

Cover design by Alex Diaz. Text design by Kim Hudgins and Alex Diaz.

☺ This paper meets the requirements of ANSI/NISO Z39.48-1992 (Permanence of Paper).

Printed in the United States of America

29 28 27 26 25   5 4 3 2 1

Joy has the potential to enhance our well-being. The Am erican Psychological Association defines joy as "a feeling of extreme gladness, delight, or exaltation of the spirit arising from a sense of wellbeing or satisfaction." What might happen if we planted more joy in our libraries and in ourselves? Library joy is more than a feeling; it is a choice that can create connection, empowerment, and wellbeing.

Within these pages, you'll find fun and practical tools to build joy-centering approaches and activities I call Library Joy Seeds. These seeds are a metaphor for the real-life joy that library staff plant every day for themselves, their communities, and the world.

Whether you are new to libraries or an experienced leader, here are 101 new ways to have fun and identify your own positive impact.

WRITE A

gratitude list

OF 10 ACTIVITIES, PEOPLE, OR THINGS

that make you smile

and refer to it often.

○ ○○ ○○ ○

1

HOST A PICNIC,

have lunch in the
sunshine,

OR SHARE A MEAL
WITH YOUR COWORKERS.

STRETCH
YOUR ARMS,
Smile
AND GIVE YOURSELF A
HUG.

Reflect on the

CALM

of being near

WATER.

DRINK SOME,

and celebrate it as part of
your self-care routine.

Assemble a virtual memento board,

AND INVITE COWORKERS AND RETIREES

to share their memories and photos.

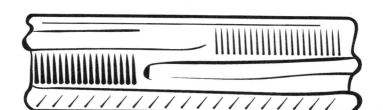

Fill a jar

WITH SMALL THINGS

that inspire you.

Add a ticket stub,
a stone,
a feather,
or a doodle.

Go down a rabbit hole

online or in a database

AND DISCOVER WAYS OTHER CULTURES

experience libraries.

(Some libraries distribute books on camels!)

PLACE A MEMENTO

OR SOUVENIR

somewhere
you will

SEE IT

WHEN YOU NEED A

pick-me-up.

9

INTRODUCE TWO OF YOUR JOY BUDDIES TO EACH OTHER.

Maybe they're regular patrons, community advocates, or coworkers.

After the library doors close,

PUT ON SOME *music,*

M O V E

AND ENCOURAGE YOUR COWORKERS

to join in the fun.

Pull something from your closet

you love

AND WEAR IT TO WORK.

Is it polka dots, a silly scarf, or something cozy?

Take
5 MINUTES

TO IMAGINE THE LIBRARY OF YOUR HEART'S DESIRE.

What do you see, hear, or smell in this space?

13

Explore the cozy Danish concept of

HYGGE

by bringing a bit of
nature inside,

noticing
soft
textures,

and drinking a
warm beverage.

PLAN AN OUTING THIS WEEK.

TAKE A

SCENIC WALK.

Pick a favorite tree in your neighborhood to read under.

Go to a restaurant with a friend.

ENCOURAGE SOMEONE
TODAY!

SEND A SHOUT-OUT
to a coworker, a customer, or a community advocate.

WRITE A BULLETED LIST

or craft a vision board

USING THE PROMPT

"THERE IS JOY IN . . .

HANG IT UP OR SAVE IT

so you can refer to it often.

17

SCHEDULE A

celebration

THIS MONTH:

COMMEMORATE A

PERSONAL,

TEAM,

or community win.

18

Send a thank-you note or text

to someone who has supported you lately.

LIST 3 WAYS YOU POSITIVELY IMPACT THE LIBRARY.

Save a copy to read when you need motivation or file it away for your annual review.

Practice self-compassion.

THINK OF
encouraging words
YOU WOULD SAY TO A FRIEND

and say these same words
TO YOURSELF INSTEAD.

Nourish plants.

Support community-shared agriculture, gardens, houseplants, or landscaping.

Learn about ecological initiatives happening with libraries.

Have a

library
JOY
day!

PUT UP SIGNS

so customers can join in the fun.

Rest and reset.

Take a short nap,
sit in the sun,
or unplug
for a while.

HONOR YOUR
COWORKERS!

MAKE AN

Award Certificate

OR BUTTON

to celebrate them.

SHARE SMALL WINS

on a bulletin board,
in a team chat,

or at a staff meeting.

IDENTIFY HOW YOUR BODY EXPERIENCES JOY.

Maybe it's a feeling of warmth in your chest or relaxation in your shoulders.

wiggle

YOUR TOES,
FINGERS,
or nose

IN A LITTLE DANCE PARTY OF ONE.

28

MAKE SPACE FOR

TRANSITIONS

between work activities.

Schedule time between meetings

and take deep breaths between tasks.

PLAY WITH WORDS!

Make a list of words that resonate with you and try writing a haiku.

Designate a daily ritual as a
JOY PRACTICE.

Maybe it's
drinking a cup of coffee
or going on a daily walk.

For a boost today,

take a deep breath,
LOWER YOUR SHOULDERS,

SMILE,

and sway!

APPRECIATE THE BEAUTY OF NATURE.

Look at the sky

AND COUNT AS MANY CLOUDS OR STARS AS YOU CAN.

TRY BIRDWATCHING

OR HIKING.

PRACTICE ACTIVE LISTENING.

Notice an individual's variations in tone, word choice, and cadence.

TAKE FULL ADVANTAGE
of your breaks and mealtimes.

CHOOSE A FEW HEALTHY FOODS
YOU ENJOY

and eat them often.

SPEND 2 MINUTES

journaling

about joyful moments
from this week.

Taking note of joy helps it grow.

Appreciate
the different textures of your workspace.

NOTICE THE FABRIC OF YOUR CLOTHING,

THE ROUGH EDGES OF BOOK BINDINGS,

or the smoothness of a keyboard.

Craft a

Playlist of

FEEL-GOOD SONGS

AND LISTEN TO IT

when you need a pick-me-up.

• • •

SHARE IT

with a
coworker.

GATHER IMAGES

that make you smile.

SAVE THEM ON YOUR PHONE

or post them on a bulletin board.

Set an intention
for the day, week, or month.

Keep it simple
and revisit it regularly.

CREATE YOUR OWN

phone or computer

BACKGROUND

using favorite

PHOTOS,

ARTWORK

OR QUOTES.

gadget

OR OFFICE SUPPLY

that makes you smile.

A DUCK-SHAPED ERASER,

A BLUE STRESS BALL,

or a new box of crayons.

List three spaces in your library
THAT YOU APPRECIATE

such as a special
book nook,
a break space,
or a cozy corner.

Choose one to visit today.

Laugh

with a coworker!

SHARE A LIBRARY JOKE,

meme,

OR
SILLY
STORY.

LOOK AT ALL THE AMAZING COLORS

in your workspace.

Think of a color that
brings you

joy

and go on a scavenger hunt

TO FIND THAT COLOR AROUND YOU.

WRITE DOWN

a quote

THAT INSPIRES YOU

and place it somewhere

you will
see it
often.

SET A

5 minute timer

for a screen-free break.

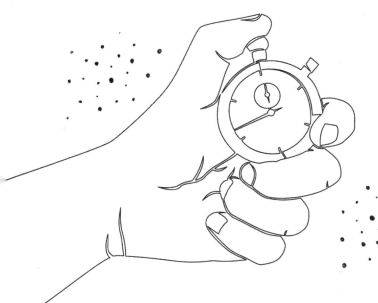

Doodle in a notebook,

take deep breaths,

OR BROWSE A BOOKLIST.

with a smile

TO YOURSELF, A SERVICE WORKER,

A STRANGER,

or a coworker.

MINDFULLY
drink a beverage.

slow down,

NOTICE THE
TEMPERATURE,

and taste
the flavors.

49

BRING VISUAL MAGIC

to your workspace. Hang a picture of a place you love, *buy a fun stapler,* or put up an inspirational quote.

Identify activities

that help you get into a creative flow

and add one

TO YOUR SCHEDULE THIS WEEK.

Try cooking, gardening, hiking,

gaming, practicing yoga,

PAINTING, OR CRAFTING.

Plan a relaxing
evening.

Keep things simple,

and fill it with ease.

Write a "done" list

WITH **3** ACCOMPLISHMENTS

YOU'RE PROUD OF

from your work journey

IN THE LAST MONTH.

Enhance your environment
WITH A NEW SCENT.

Use a diffuser, apply a new lotion, or incorporate aromatherapy oils.

Lean toward a beginner's mind and

TRY SOMETHING NEW

at a library—

A NEW SOFTWARE,
webinar,
or resource.

Grab a bag,

NAME IT YOUR

"Joy-to-Go bag,"

and fill it with

photos, cards, or a stress ball.

Practice loving-kindness meditation

by thinking of someone who has supported you
and saying these phrases:

"May you be happy.

May you be well.

May you be peaceful and at ease."

Make a mind map!

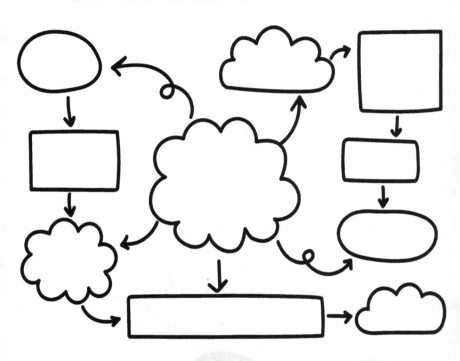

ADD WORDS, PHRASES, OR DRAWINGS
TO VISUALIZE FRIENDS, TRAVEL,
cooking, outdoors, and the arts.

WRITE A LIST OF

PEOPLE

you can connect with

{ WHEN YOU NEED A HUG }

(real or virtual),

PEP TALK,

or a reminder of what's true.

SCHEDULE time to SHADOW someone who INSPIRES your work.

Spend time with
animals

or ask your coworkers
about pets in their lives.

Try knitting or another fiber art.

Bring a skein of yarn and a pair of needles for breaks or lunch.

Find a crafting buddy.

Consider 3 skills

you could further develop
to support your work.

Then, take an action to further one of the skills:

sign up for a class, webinar,
an informational interview,
or coaching.

CERTIFICATE

LOOK UP THE
feelings wheel

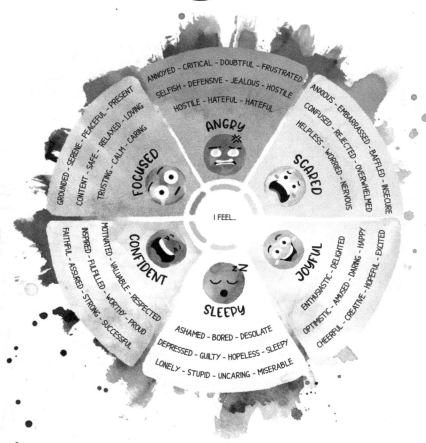

ANNOYED - CRITICAL - DOUBTFUL - FRUSTRATED
SELFISH - DEFENSIVE - JEALOUS - HOSTILE
HOSTILE - HATEFUL - HATEFUL

ANGRY

GROUNDED - SERENE - PEACEFUL - PRESENT
CONTENT - SAFE - RELAXED - LOVING
TRUSTING - CALM - CARING

FOCUSED

ANXIOUS - EMBARRASSED - BAFFLED - INSECURE
CONFUSED - REJECTED - OVERWHELMED
HELPLESS - WORRIED - NERVOUS

SCARED

I FEEL...

FAITHFUL - ASSURED - STRONG - SUCCESSFUL
INSPIRED - FULFILLED - WORTHY - PROUD
MOTIVATED - VALUABLE - RESPECTED

CONFIDENT

SLEEPY

JOYFUL

ENTHUSIASTIC - DELIGHTED
OPTIMISTIC - AMUSED - DARING - HAPPY
CHEERFUL - CREATIVE - HOPEFUL - EXCITED

ASHAMED - BORED - DESOLATE
DEPRESSED - GUILTY - HOPELESS - SLEEPY
LONELY - STUPID - UNCARING - MISERABLE

AND EXPLORE THE RANGE OF
positive emotions
IN IT.

Consider

WHAT MIGHT STILL BRING YOU JOY

IN FIVE YEARS' TIME.

HOW MIGHT YOU
give those things energy

TODAY?

Leave your work

AT WORK!

Turn notifications off

AND PRACTICE SETTING

CLEAR BOUNDARIES

FOR YOURSELF.

FIND A LIBRARY CAUSE

that resonates with you

AND SUPPORT IT TODAY.

SPREAD AWARENESS ON SOCIAL MEDIA,
mention it to a friend,
or sign up to volunteer.

Create a
film noir-
inspired
photo
of your
library.

Set your
camera
to black and
white, use
low lighting,
and amplify
the shadows
you see.

Display your
mysterious creation.

a quick massage

–your face, neck, shoulders, or hands.

MAKE A
PAPER AIRPLANE

AND TRY FLYING IT

around your workspace.

SAVOR the current season.

LOOK for active wildlife.

TASTE a seasonal vegetable or fruit.

SPEND time outdoors.

71

REFLECT ON FUN ACTIVITIES FROM YOUR CHILDHOOD

and pick one to incorporate into your week.

SCRIBBLE WITH CRAYONS,

sing in the shower, or visit a playground.

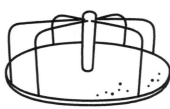

SIMPLIFY WORK WHERE YOU CAN:

MAKE ROUTINES,
tackle challenging tasks earlier in the day,

 create checklists,
DELETE APPS,
edit your closet,

AND LIMIT YOUR OPTIONS.

Look up various librarians
ON SCREEN.

PICK ONE TO WATCH,

such as *Desk Set*, a classic from the 1950s.

CHAMPION

your community's
entrepreneurs and artists.

Invite them to share their story
with your library–

maybe through staff training,
a book recommendation,

or collaborating
on a local exhibit.

75

Make an
ALPHABET SCAVENGER HUNT

where you take a photo of a
place, object, or person

for each letter of the alphabet.

MAKE A

Wish List

1. _____
2. _____
3. _____

. . . .
of three things
you would do at work
if you could.

SHARE IT WITH YOUR SUPERVISOR.

Walk around the physical perimeter of your library.

NOTICE SOMETHING NEW ABOUT THIS SPACE.

JOT DOWN A MANTRA
OR AFFIRMATION
AND ADD IT TO YOUR WORKSPACE

or Joy-to-Go bag.

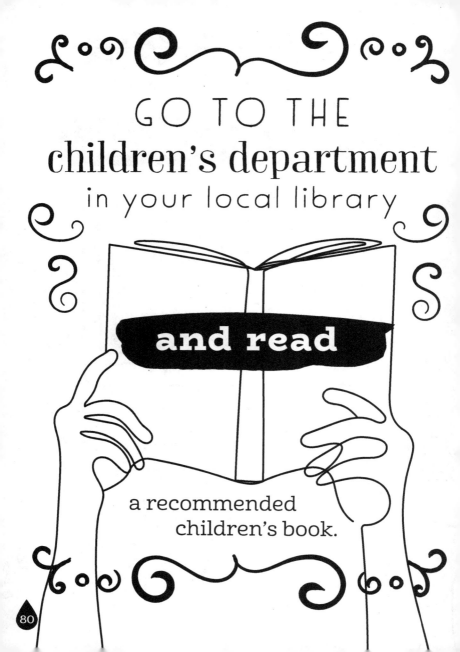

GO TO THE
children's department
in your local library

and read

a recommended
children's book.

Find a local bulletin board or online message board and notice positive things happening in your community.

IDEA!

For You!

Meeting

TO DO LIST

OK!

today at 5 p.m.

THROW A
BARBEQUE
OR COMMUNITY PICNIC

TO CELEBRATE
LIBRARY CARD SIGNUP
MONTH.

Adventure
to a new
PARK
or
**GREEN
SPACE**
near your
work.

SHARE SNACKS
with library staff

in gratitude
AND CONNECTION.

PRACTICE CREATIVE PROBLEM-SOLVING ON A WORK CHALLENGE.

Looking to bring more **teens** into libraries?

ASK TEENS TO JOIN IN ON THE BRAINSTORMING!

Practice responding with **"yes, and"** instead of **"no, but."**

TRY THE "5 WHYS" APPROACH.

Take your lunch outside.

Find a bench,
    picnic table, or a
cozy spot in the grass.

Create something

FEEL-GOOD HORMONES.

Cook a new recipe, write a poem, or sew a tote bag.

87

Browse

a library collection
or resource.

Flip through the pages

of books that jump out to you.

EXPLORE
A NEW PODCAST

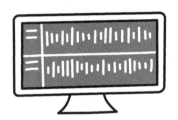

or watch
a video

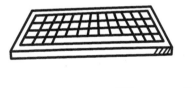

TO SPARK
YOUR
CURIOSITY.

Rest your eyes.

Take screen breaks and focus your
gaze on an item across the room
or outside a window.

Whistle, hum, or sing WHILE CLEANING OR OR TIDYING UP YOUR WORKSPACE.

REMINISCE ABOUT A BOOK THAT YOU'VE enjoyed reading recently.

Post a book recommendation for it in your staff workroom or share it with a coworker.

Strike up a conversation

WITH SOMEONE NEW IN YOUR

WORK WORLD.

WHAT IS BRINGING THEM

joy lately?

LOOK AT YOUR WORK MESSAGES

and identify a buddy you haven't connected with lately and

REACH OUT TO THEM.

ARRANGE A SILLY SOCK CONTEST AT WORK.

REWARD THE WINNER WITH A FUN TREAT.

95

Be a

VIRTUAL

library tourist.

AL-QARAWIYYIN LIBRARY 🔍

Check out the Al-Qarawiyyin Library, the oldest, continuously running library in the world in Fez, Morocco!

LINCOLN'S POCKETS 🔍

Discover the contents of Lincoln's pockets by searching the Library of Congress collection!

FIND A POSITIVE OR SILLY

NEWS STORY

AND SHARE IT WITH A

COWORKER.

Schedule positive activities in your calendar this week–

breathwork,

birdwatching,

or volunteering.

Even 5 minutes daily supports wellness.

Pay it forward with a random act of kindness.

Go outside or open a window.

Embrace the sound of a birdsong,
the feeling of a cool breeze,
or whatever nature you encounter.

The poet Toi Derricotte wrote,

JOY IS AN ACT OF RESISTANCE.

Journal about how your joy is,

OR COULD BE, AN ACT OF *Resistance.*

Sources

Library Joy Seeds have been inspired by the work of many sources, including the following advocates, researchers, and writers.

Audrey Barbakoff
Barbara Biziou
Anna Brones
adrienne maree brown
Brené Brown
Tarana Burke
Laurie J. Cameron
Elfreda Chatman
Deb Dana
Jamila Dugan
Ingrid Fetell Lee
Susie Ghahremani
Marlee Grace
Morgan Harper Nichols
Stephanie Harrison
Prentis Hemphill
Liz Lamoreux

Jen Lara
Noah Lenstra
Alina Liao
Jenn Lim
LeeAnn Mallorie
Araba Maze
Amelia Nagoski
Emily Nagoski
Kristin Neff
Priya Parker
Robin Raven
Euphemia Russell
Martin Seligman
Sonya Renee Taylor
Mychal Threets
Karen Walrond
Meik Wiking

Resources

Amabile, Teresa M., and Steven J. Kramer. 2011. "The Power of Small Wins." *Harvard Business Review*. https://hbr.org/2011/05/the-power-of-small-wins.

APA Dictionary of Psychology. s.v., "joy." https://dictionary.apa.org/joy.

Creative Education Foundation. "What Is Creative Problem Solving?" www.creativeeducationfoundation.org/what-is-cps/.

Dericotte, Toi. 2008. "Joy Is an Act of Resistance, and: Special Ears, and: Another poem of a small grieving for my fish Telly, and: On the reasons I loved Telly the Fish." *Prairie Schooner* 82, no. 3: 22. https://doi.org/10.1353/psg.0.0107.

Evans, Clark. *What Was in Lincoln's Pockets?* From Library of Congress, Hidden Treasures at the Library of Congress, video. www.loc.gov/item/myloc16/.

Fry, Tatiana. 2021. "Al-Qarawiyyin: University, Library, and Mosque in One." Bright Insight, May 14. https://access.the brightcontinent.org/items/show/28.

IMDb. "Desk Set." www.imdb.com/title/tt0050307/.

"Loving-Kindness Meditation with Sharon Salzberg." Mindful. www
.mindful.org/loving-kindness-meditation-with-sharon-salzberg/.